The Front-Line Manager

Practical Advice for Success

The Front-Line Manager
Practical Advice for Success

Omi–Kooch–Ka Publishing
Ottawa, Canada
www.omi-kooch-ka.com

Author: Angela Tyler

© 2022 by Angela Tyler – all rights reserved

No part of this book may be reproduced, stored in a retrieval system, or transmitted by any means without the written permission of the author

ISBN: Paperback 978-1-7775383-6-1
ISBN: e-Book 978-1-7775383-7-8

Cover Photograph: Sarah Hum – Used with permission.

CONTENTS

PREFACE vii

PART ONE: Moving Forward and Implementing Change   1

PART TWO: Managing Staff for Positive Results   21

PART THREE: Leadership Qualities   36

PART FOUR: Personal Development   50

CONCLUSION   61

PREFACE

I wrote this book to highlight practical aspects of management you can use to help succeed as a front-line manager. I saw the difference various approaches make in managing people and how they set the stage for organizations to learn from problems and mistakes, enabling them to improve, and continue to grow.

One of my earliest experiences was to be responsible for three research laboratories containing fifteen or so researchers. I learned a lot from the many challenges I faced.

When I first began, I would bring my concerns to my supervisor, often pointing out areas requiring improvement. Every time, the response was "so what are you going to do about it?" This made me feel rather annoyed! Instead of accepting responsibility, he refused, and made me take responsibility for them. He did, however, give me the flexibility, trust, and time, needed to address, solve, and make the necessary improvements.

It is through experiences like this and many others that I came to believe that flexible, dynamic, and productive organizations are made by acknowledging and solving problems. Doing so will lead to a culture of continuous improvement.

This book will provide you with practical lessons to be an effective leader, as a front-line manager. It is organized around four areas that are critical to performing at the level of a leader.

PART ONE

MOVING FORWARD AND IMPLEMENTING CHANGE

What Does it Mean to be a Manager?

Manager Definition

A manager is a person who is responsible for managing people, processes, and resources. They are responsible for a variety of tasks such as conflict resolution, problem solving, performance appraisals, implementing or improving upon processes and standard operating procedures. Managers in short, are responsible for the smooth functioning of an organization.

Three Types of Managers

The three main types of managers are:

1. Senior Manager – President, Chief Executive Officer (CEO), Executive Vice-President.

2. Middle Manager – Departmental Head, Division Head, and Directors.

3. Front-line Manager – Supervisor, Office Manager, etc.

The focus of this book is on the front-line manager; however, all managerial roles are incredibly important. In small organizations and companies, it is not uncommon for managers to be responsible for two or even play all three management roles.

Additional Terminology:

Organization: the term "organization" is used to represent a government program, private or public company, a non-profit, or branch.

Understand and Acknowledge Your Worth

Where To Start: Are you a senior front-line manager, a junior manager, or a person who aspires to become one? In either case, you need to understand the importance of your role. You are, or will be, in a position of leadership, placing you in a role of responsibility. The front-line is where people put their

Moving Forward and Implementing Change

talents and time into implementation. Accordingly, value your worth and those to whom you give supervision.

Experience has shown me it is very important for the frontline manager to know and understand the organization's purpose, objectives, and strategy. You also need to align employees so that these are shared equally with them. Accordingly, accurate internal knowledge must be communicated and taken into consideration in every aspect of your planning and implementation.

Often, hiring managers overlook the need to provide adequate information on the purpose and goals of their organization. Research on your part, including discussions with others, will likely be needed.

Educate yourself on the expectations of upper management. Are there plans for growth or are they planning to maintain the status quo. Carefully thinking through where the organization is today and where they want to be, is important. This will put you on a firm foundation on your path forward and will allow you to manage more effectively.

The next step is to clearly understand what and how things are currently being done to achieve the purpose and mandate of your organization. Should you be new to the area, learn as much as you can, then apply critical thinking and analysis to current methods and practices. This will help you to make a judgement on the effectiveness of current practices.

Once your understanding is clear on the company's objectives, using your analysis, you can begin the process of breaking down the individual tasks and processes. You can either accept them as is or come up with innovative steps to recommend and develop.

Moving Forward and Implementing Change

If you have ideas that you believe would result in increased efficiency, consider sharing them with your management. However, any proposed changes should be discussed with sensitivity as some individuals may be easily threatened.

> *I would like to highlight the importance of asking questions concerning change management during interviews. If you feel you would be working in an environment that is not open to change, you should take this into consideration when deciding to accept an offer of employment.*

> *Working in an environment not open to change often leads to frustration and stress.*

An often-occurring problem is when a new manager taking over from a previous manager, assumes that the established steps and processes currently in place are effective and efficient. Part of your analysis would be to take the time to follow the processes and steps to identify those that are redundant, areas that need improvement, and noting what is working correctly. It is common to ask an employee why they perform a task only to receive the response, "because this is the way I was told to do it." Even if something is not working properly or is unnecessary, individuals may continue with the same method as it is familiar to them, based on how they were taught.

To fill the role of an efficient front-line manager, you should allow and encourage your employees to question what, why, and how they work, and give them an opportunity to express their opinions. This will allow them to realize they are valued as individuals and their contributions are meaningful.

Moving Forward and Implementing Change

To succeed in your role as manager, it is important that you look at the processes as a whole and understand how each part interacts within the context of the whole.

The goal is always to bring about a desired outcome while valuing your employees, meeting the objectives and goals of your organization, and working with efficiency.

Story: One Spring, we received little precipitation. Over time, my concern for people who rely on rain, such as farmers and those living from wells, had grown. During a conversation with a friend, I mentioned my concern for the lack of rain. She responded with "Why, don't you have a hose?" She saw the issue through her own needs and not the bigger picture.

Often, how we focus on an issue can result in small box thinking. It is important to step back and keep the 'big picture' in view. For example, my view of the lack of precipitation would lead to ideas of solving food production issues. Would we have to import more food, or would there be food inflation causing problems for all?

My friend was asking me if I had a hose. This gave me an answer to cope with the lack of rain in my yard. However, it did not cover the larger issues.

Create a Culture of Continuous Improvement

Internal Communications

As a new front-line manager or, as mentioned earlier, an existing manager, it is important before making any changes to follow the processes and, also the communication flow within and between personnel. Once completed, you will be able to identify how processes are understood by your employees and if they are efficient.

Their knowledge, as well as your own observations, will help you identify areas that are perceived to need attention. This exercise will also provide you time to see each employee as an individual and get to know them better.

This analysis will assist you in identifying areas that require improvement or those that could be further developed. Writing down your observations and ideas will help you remember them. In addition, be receptive to ideas from your employees.

Once you are feeling confident with the ideas for improvement, consider bringing them to the attention of your supervisor but as mentioned previously, with sensitivity. Don't forget to give credit to individuals who provided good ideas.

Once you are granted permission from management to proceed with new ideas, you will have an exciting opportunity to show your worth. The first impulse is to start implementing changes right away. However, this might not be a time for change but a time of continued learning.

Moving Forward and Implementing Change

Once you have spent time getting to know your employees and you feel confident it is time to start making changes, do so gradually.

I found that starting with something simple is the place to start. Choose something that will not take a lot of time but will have maximum positive impact. Remember, gaining trust and acceptance from your employees happens over time.

Through experience I have learned that a manager who makes changes too quickly runs the risk of ending up with a hostile and unhappy group. On the other hand, if no changes are made, employees will become intolerant to change and therefore little to no growth will occur. Always remember that changes which impact your employees directly, must be undertaken carefully with explanations that allow for open discussion.

For ongoing improvements, it is helpful to develop a list of areas where you would like changes to occur, including those that were brought to your attention by your employees.

I believe a new manager after becoming familiar with the employees and the culture, will arrive at a point where they can use their instincts to decide what is the most important task to engage in next.

Importance of Follow-up

After new processes or steps are introduced or improved upon, make sure to follow-up with your employees to see what is working and if something needs to be further adjusted. Rarely are changes perfect the first time. Follow-up after each adjustment.

A front-line manager cannot assume if no one complains everything is fine. Use your staff meetings to encourage open discussions. Also, be open to feedback from your employees on a daily basis.

Using Consultants

There will likely be times when consultants are needed to address a specific subject where more information is required. They can also be used to help identify and resolve internal problems in your workplace. This could be undertaken, especially, when serious changes might be the result.

However, I have heard that recommendations from consultants often fail to achieve the desired outcome. This, I would argue, is due to the fact consultants typically are not hired to stay to implement the changes. Knowing what needs to be done is only half of the solution. Being able to implement and follow up until the desired outcome is achieved takes time.

Example: A company having difficulty with employee engagement decides that they need to find out why. Their employees lack interest, motivation, and are often taking extra long breaks and lunches. The owner of the company decides to hire an external consultant to investigate the problem and come up with recommendations to solve the issues.

1. A Consultant comes and organizes meetings with management and the employees. The first meeting consists of meeting managers, they explain their expectations and how they see the process unfolding as set out in the Terms of Reference.

Moving Forward and Implementing Change

2. Individual meetings with employees and managers take place ensuring the consultant receives input from everyone. People process information differently, and need time to reflect and think, therefore employees need to be advised that any additional information can be sent to the consultant by email.

3. With the information received through file research, meetings, and emails, an analysis is completed, and a report written by the consultant, who sets out the findings.

4. This report is then given to the owner and or senior level management.

5. The consultant, having completed his job, is paid and leaves.

An organization lacking a follow up plan to address the issues discovered by the consultant, will not likely proceed further. This whole undertaking could end up being a waste of time and resources.

Thinking Strategically

The consultant can be further employed to develop an implementation plan, or it could be decided that you as the front-line manager, using the consultant's advice, should develop the implementation plan. Upon approval, you could then proceed with its implementation.

Moving Forward and Implementing Change

A well thought out action plan that addresses the main issues, implements changes, and follows up to determine the impact on the organization must be the ultimate outcome.

For more information on change management, there are excellent books published on this topic.

Change Happens Gradually Over Time

Once you, and or your employees, have identified areas that need improvement, select the areas where there is high consensus from your employees. Changes, as mentioned previously, that make a noticeable improvement for your employees will build up trust for bigger changes in the future. Also, do not expect perfection overnight. Change may happen more gradually than what you expect. This will require you as the manager to be patient with the change process.

Story: The story of the invention of the television is both entertaining, interesting, and noteworthy. No one single person developed the television but several individuals over time.

From The Book of Popular Science, 1929 – Volume 15, page 5328, there is a passage I think is excellent: "A distant person can be seen and easily recognized, his motions can be followed as, for instance, he turns the pages of a magazine, and it is stated that even the pictures in the magazine can be seen as the subject himself looks at them.

Of course, at present, all this is still in a somewhat underdeveloped stage, the apparatus is complicated and expensive, and the commercial applications are not as yet very evident. But judging from the progress of the telephone, the radio, the phonograph, etc., the day will doubtless come when we shall look upon television with no more curiosity than we now do upon them."

In this example, progress occurred over time, little by little. If these individuals were risk aversive, our lives would certainly be different from what it is today.

Changes and Risk

We are living in a society where companies and organizations realize that change is often highly correlated with increased risks. They are often, however, forced to move quickly due to changing environments and technology. Although change usually does mean increasing one's risk, I believe, it is through risk and change that we can move more effectively into the dynamic fast changing environment that we currently face.

The following page consists of questions that will help you as a front-line manager draw upon your own experiences. Bringing your expectations and perceived outcomes forward will enable you to move more effectively with change.

QUESTIONS FOR REFLECTION
Your Experience with Changes in the Workplace

1. Looking back over your career, have you experienced changes that had a major impact on a key aspect of your work or workplace environment?

2. What were the type of changes, and how were you affected personally? How did the changes affect your colleagues?

3. How were the changes announced and implemented?

4. With hindsight, was there specific aspects that could have been handled more effectively?

Clearly Define Roles and Responsibilities

Your Skilled Employees

Personally, I find the task of defining roles and responsibilities has become more challenging in recent years. I say this because it seems every industry is undergoing change from the implementation of new processes, new technologies, evolving priorities, and mandate. Change is occurring both at the operational and management levels.

Due to this growth challenge, it is important to cultivate a group of employees with a diverse skill set, and who are flexible. You may even need to consider switching roles around among the employees to achieve this.

Each time there is a major change, it is imperative that you as the manager pay careful attention to employees who are affected. Ensure the changes function with current processes and employees to produce the desired outcome.

There is a possibility that you may need to identify and modify current roles and responsibilities and, if necessary, create new roles entirely.

It is important to note that if you add people or additional tasks to an inefficient process, it makes things worse, not better.

Standard Operating Procedures

Many tasks often require specific attention to detail. Engineers, accountants, architects, electricians, plumbing, and construction all require strict attention to work according to specified standards. Therefore, you must ask the question,

"Will standard operating procedures (SOPs) help in your particular environment?"

The SOPs will ensure that steps required to carry out a particular task are consistent. They also make training easier. However, your SOPs should be reviewed annually to determine if they need to be updated in our fast-changing world.

Also, one must be aware that they can reduce creativity and bring boredom to the task. Accordingly, they must be used wisely in areas where precision is required.

Provide Clear Instructions

Providing clear instructions is important. Instructions that are not clear can lead to unnecessary stress and wasted time. Here is a simple example: This is your first day on the job, and you have been given the task of taking out the garbage. You are told – 'we usually collect the trash when the garbage cans are around two thirds full or smell'. This instruction would leave you always second guessing when you should remove the trash. Instead, the following instructions would provide structure and allow the new employee to develop a routine:

'The garbage is collected Tuesdays and Fridays'.

What to Accept and Expect from Employees

People are very different. Some like instructions, others do not. As a front-line manager, you have a responsibility to relate directly with employees and provide them with instructions as well as feedback and correction if necessary.

Moving Forward and Implementing Change

Your reason for managing is first and foremost to achieve the outcome set by your management.

Your role is to respect people and treat them with dignity and respect. This includes management as well as staff.

If an employee lacks the skillset to fulfill a needed role, you have three choices: 1) Retrain for the same position. 2) Move to a different position having a more suitable skill set or 3) fire the employee.

If you have a Human Resources (HR) Unit, ask them for assistance. Remember, should the decision be made to fire the employee, it is not always a bad outcome. Working in an area where one's personality and skill set are wrong is certainly not in the best interest of the person or for the organization.

Performance Appraisals

Most employees require and appreciate feedback on how their contributions are being perceived by you as their manager. Many organizations have developed the custom of giving annual performance appraisals. Performance appraisals, however, must be taken seriously and given the time needed to ensure a comprehensive and fair approach. To be fully effective, each employee should have an interview opportunity to discuss their evaluation with you. Should an employee be struggling, this would give you the opportunity for finding the root cause of the problem.

Moving Forward and Implementing Change

Goals and Key Performance Indicators

Every organization, no matter its purpose, has perceived outcomes. A front-line manager must be aware of what these perceived outcomes are. They differ depending on the established objectives.

For example, a retail store will be focused on revenue and number of items sold. A not-for-profit organization with the objective of providing shelter for individuals who find themselves homeless, would be interested in tracking the number of individuals requiring shelter, the capacity of the shelter, number of adults and children sheltered, number of individuals turned away, etc.

Key performance indicators (KPIs) are quantifiable measures that can be used to track performance based on the goals of your unique company. Should these be missing, work toward developing them with upper management, as all management must agree with them.

KPIs are used to track the work unit's productivity and can be used to ensure individual employee's goals are being achieved. The bottom line is to know, with certainty, what goals are required to achieve "success".

Setting goals that are in alignment with the company's mandate will keep the focus on improvement and growth. However, remember that some KPIs are easier to measure than others. KPIs must be fully understood by employees, if not, they will not be measured effectively or not at all.

Moving Forward and Implementing Change

Example: At a clothing boutique, management wants to increase their annual revenue by 15%, increase the number of dresses sold by 10%, and increase the number of visitors to the store by 20%.

Having written goals, shared with all employees, and measurable, significantly increases the probability that management and employees will focus on how to achieve them.

For the clothing boutique example, the goals can be quantitatively measured using the key performance indicators:
1. Total revenue.
2. Number of dresses sold.
3. Visitor count

If the goals are annually based, record the KPIs monthly. This provides time to adjust and modify strategies if the measures are below the set goals. Similarly, if the goals are monthly, record measures on a weekly basis.

Additionally, to say we are going to increase our sales by 15% without providing actual numbers makes measuring the progress vague and difficult.

Clothing Boutique – Number of Dresses Sold
(1st Quarter)

	Jan	Feb	March	Quarterly
Goal	125	125	125	375
Actual	95	115	130	340
Strategy			Sale (Mar 1-7)	
	Google Ad	Google Ad	Google Ad	
Ideas for next month		Sale, update website	Update display area, research fashion trends	
% To goal				90.7 %

Given the time of year is winter, they are doing well on meeting their sales goal for dresses. During the first quarter, they have managed to reach close to their goal.

Make It Fun!

Reaching a goal can be rewarded with something the employees will enjoy. For example, the manager can promise to buy pizza for lunch if the goal is reached. This is a fun way to acknowledge the achievement. The group lunch also provides an excellent opportunity to discuss the processes that brought them to reach their goal and discuss ideas moving forward.

Moving Forward and Implementing Change

QUESTIONS FOR REFLECTION

Goals and Key Performance Indicators for the Work Unit

1. Do you have goals indicating what your work unit should accomplish in the next twelve months?

2. Describe the process taken within your organization to establish goals for your work unit.

3. Is there an opportunity for you to provide input in setting goals? Do your employees have an opportunity to provide input?

4. Do you currently track key performance indicators?

5. How are the key performance indicators aligned with your work unit goals?

SUMMARY: PART ONE

- Develop a clear understanding of your organization's mandate, its objectives, and its desired output.
- Build and sustain confidence and trust.
- Encourage employees to ask questions on how they work.
- Consider change opportunities – proceed with caution.
- Limit the amount of change occurring at any given time.
- Follow up on changes – rarely is anything perfect the first time.
- Keep track of your unit's progress over time.
- Assign clear roles, responsibilities, and expectations.
- Hire to build a diversified skill set.
- Establish what to accept and expect from employees.
- Undertake performance appraisals for your staff.
- Establish monthly and/or annual goals.
- Measure goals using key performance indicators.

PART TWO

MANAGING STAFF FOR POSITIVE RESULTS

Every Task is Important

Tasks

Management

Employees

Company Direction

The Wheel Theory of Importance

From experience, I came to see the overall importance of managers, employees, and tasks, as a wheel. Upper management determines what, why, and how of the organization, and its desired outputs. This will include a strategy on where the organization is heading. Once the strategy is known, middle managers along with the front-line managers can then determine the resources and processes required to achieve the outputs.

As the wheel diagram suggests, all parts of the wheel must work together. The solid centre are the clearly defined objectives as defined by its senior managers. Without a solid centre (clearly defined objectives) the wheel's journey becomes uncertain. An organization, program, etc. can have an incredible team but without a solid core, the organization can go in the wrong direction entirely or find its direction uncertain and changing without due cause.

The front-line manager has the responsibility to assign tasks to their employees to get optimal outputs. It is very important the front-line manager realizes that all tasks are important. Every job, at all levels, will likely contain tasks that are more routine, not overly exciting, or prestigious. It is therefore easy to overlook the importance of these tasks. Looking at the wheel idea, if one task (or spoke) is undertaken improperly, the wheel still might function and not fail. However, should more of the spokes become bent and stop supporting the outer wheel, this then starts to affect the wheel. The wheel starts to wobble. It is important, as the front-line-manager, to work with your employees to identify problems and solve them. Doing this on an ongoing basis will improve the organization, keep it strong, and uncompromised.

Story: I once presented the Wheel Theory of Importance to a group of researchers. If you are in science, you will already appreciate the high level of routine and not prestigious tasks that are required daily.

The next day, one of the young researchers was humming along the corridor with a bag requiring autoclaving. He stopped and told me how my talk had made a huge impact on him. Before he hated the process of autoclaving the bags of waste, but now, he understood the importance of doing so and the repercussions of not autoclaving would cause to both the employees and company.

Not every employee will grasp this idea, but for those who do, it can have enormous benefits to both their self-esteem and to the organization. In addition, if a manager can view each job or task as important, their employees will also see them as important and will take greater pride in their work.

Micro-Managing

Changing Your Perspective

If you want to destroy team spirit and create a lackluster attitude where everyone simply works to get a paycheck, then you can think about micro-managing your team.

What does micro-managing mean? Micro-managing is when a manager controls every aspect of their team's actions. Managers who follow this practice are often not tolerant of anyone suggesting or making changes to their work practices.

If you want people to enjoy and be connected to their jobs, if possible, allow them to find their own way to fulfill their roles. Just remember, there is always more than one way to accomplish any given task.

Unfortunately, many managers who micromanage think they are doing a great job. Micromanaging however causes employees to become frustrated, disconnected, and overall unhappy being at work.

Examine Your Management Style

Do you feel your team could not operate without you? If you suspect you might be a micromanager, talk with your team, and ask if they see you as one.

If they say yes, discuss with them ways in which you could relax your control over their work. To recover from this sort of relationship, requires ongoing and open communication. However difficult, this is well worth doing and will improve the relationship over time.

It is easy to fall into this practice of micromanaging when you come across an employee who lacks the necessary skills to perform their duties sufficiently. Doing so often results in frustration for both you and the employee. Could this underperformance be linked with your style of management? Are you micromanaging to a point where creativity is decreased and the cause for employees becoming bored and frustrated?

Instead of micro-managing, investigate with the employee any underlying problems. You might just find out that you may need to change your management style as this might be the root cause of the problem.

Another observation I made over the years is if a manager believes people around them are incompetent, their employees will over time become so. The manager's attitude is reflected in their body language, tone of voice, and their overall ability to communicate with their employees.

QUESTIONS FOR REFLECTION

Dealing with Micro-Managing

1. To what extent are there symptoms of micro-managing in your work unit? To gain further insights, research the topic further.

2. A variety of factors may be contributing to symptoms including organizational culture, your work experience, and the needs of employees. Is there a need to seek assistance from HR advisors to identify and assess factors contributing to micro-managing?

3. Are there courses that you can take to address micromanaging?

Meetings

There are several types of meetings based on their objective, such as:

- Planning
- Status update
- Decision-making
- Info-sharing
- Innovation
- Problem solving
- Performance appraisals

What are your meeting experiences? Do you currently have staff meetings, program specific meetings, or meetings for any of the other reasons listed above? Are your meetings happening on a set schedule or are they happening when there is a perceived need?

Meetings occur when there is a need to coordinate work, discuss problems or provide updates. They are important if they provide leadership and direction to the project or issue. They are extremely useful in ensuring that the group has shared objectives, goals, and an understanding of the importance of the direction in which you want to move toward.

Staff Meetings

To hold successful staff meetings, there must be a balance between providing enough direction without micromanaging your staff. Staff meetings are usually held on a regular basis,

Managing Staff for Positive Results

and can occur weekly, biweekly, or monthly. If possible, from my experience, they should preferably be held on a Friday. This gives your employees a break from their usual routine, and it gives them, including you, time to think about the discussions and issues over the weekend. Holding the meetings in the late morning or afternoon will provide you and your team time to prepare for the meeting.

Aspects of Successful Meetings:

The Agenda

The most important aspect of a meeting is the agenda. Having an agenda provides structure and a clearly defined purpose or objective. If possible, send the agenda to participants at least two days before the meeting. This provides time for individuals to reflect, request that additional items be added to the agenda, and prepare material if required.

The Chair

The purpose of the Chair is to keep discussions focused on the agenda. Their role is to prevent topics from changing course and ensuring not too much time is spent on one topic. Each agenda item requires sufficient time for discussion and attention. Unless there is a clearly perceived need to move or add another subject area, it is always better to stay focused on the agenda.

Always consider who should be the meeting Chair. They should have the ability, through their knowledge of the subject area and the participants, to move discussions along without getting the attendees annoyed or becoming bored.

Attendee Participation

It is common to have one or two individuals monopolize the meeting. Why does this occur? Not everyone at your meeting will be comfortable speaking in front of the group. Do not assume if individuals are quiet, they lack interest or are not engaged. Even if they have ideas to contribute, they may remain silent.

Make sure to mention if anyone would like to discuss an issue further with you in private, they are welcome. In addition, it is important to realize that individuals process information at different rates. Some individuals need more time and therefore, it is important that they can discuss their ideas with you later. Open door policy works wonders here!

Meeting Attendees

Another important aspect of meetings is to ensure that everyone who needs to be present, is invited to attend. This includes individuals where you need their information and input to resolve questions and advance the discussion. Also include individuals where they need information from the meeting on a firsthand basis. This is especially important for teams where members need to be both informed and actively involved in order to build a cohesive team.

Keep Specific Details to a Minimum

It is easy to go into too much detail during a meeting. To hold successful meetings, you must find the balance between providing enough direction and information to provide clarity without overloading your staff with details.

The key is to bring forward the important facts, issues, and ideas that are required to make progress on the topic. Too much detail can slow progress and lead the group to frustration instead of the desired result you want to achieve.

Meeting Minutes (Notes)

Having a clear record of meetings is important. A capable employee needs be assigned to take the minutes during meetings. The minutes should include the main discussion points and the key outcomes. This allows the Chair to do their work, while another person concentrates on the minutes.

Action Item Table

Most meetings will result in a list of action items. It is important to list them in a table to be included in the meeting minutes. Action items, however, often fail to be acted upon due to the lack of assigning tasks to individuals. This is where delegating becomes important. During the meeting, be sure to assign action items (tasks) to individuals.

Example Action Items: Team Meeting
Date: DD/MM/YYYY

Action Items	Name(s)	Expected Date of Completion	Comments	Completed? (Y/N)
Create distribution group email	Nancy Smith	June 18	Contact Ahmed for list of emails.	
Create Event Invitation	Richard Bantry	June 15		

Adding a table in the minutes that lists the action items, the person(s) responsible, and the expected date of completion is important.

Remember, A good manager delegates. They do not try to do everything themselves.

On the right-hand side of the table, have a column labeled "completed?" This informs the attendees that you will be following up before the next meeting to check mark the action items as complete.

The updated action item table could be added to your agenda for the next meeting. Visually seeing the completed tasks, the meeting participants are better able to move forward and acknowledge action items that were finished and deal with those that were not completed within the timeframe. Doing so can uncover early problems such as lack of resources, or other issues.

Special Meetings to Address Problems

Story: Working at a private company, I became aware of concerns of the employees regarding processes, lack of communication between divisions, etc. I also noticed no or almost no effort was being done to solve the issues or in making improvements.

I therefore recommended that we should begin monthly meetings to address these concerns. Next, I needed permission from the Director to allow employees time to attend. The request was accepted, and I was thrilled!

At the first meeting I was completely confused, however. The President, CEO, Directors, and all managers came to the meeting. The President stood and asked if there were any problems. What he received was a room full of blank stares and no one spoke up.

After the meeting, I went back to the Director, and asked if I could schedule another meeting, but this time, without the President or the CEO, as I felt that no one would discuss the issues in their presence. Once again, I was given permission to hold another meeting. This time, the President, CEO, and Directors did not attend but all the Managers came. The response from the employees slightly improved with a couple of people bravely speaking up. However, most of the employees stayed silent.

Once again, I went back to the Director and asked for permission to host another meeting but this time, I told him I did not want the President, CEO, Directors, or Managers attending. After some reluctance, he agreed to allow for another meeting.

At the third meeting, the response from the employees was simply incredible. It was as if they suddenly came alive and highly enthusiastic. Everyone at the meeting spoke and discussed issues. The meeting input and output was the complete opposite from the first and second meeting.

This was an important lesson on how people respond to authority figures. Something for management to seriously take into consideration.

If you feel you are having meetings to discuss problems where there is low participation, consider choosing a person who is respected by their peers to schedule, draft agendas from input from their colleagues, and host meetings.

Team Building

Having Teams that Work

Front-line managers often rely on teams to achieve specific projects. In this discussion, a team consists of two or more individuals working together to achieve a specific project.

It takes careful and thoughtful handling to create and sustain a productive and engaged team. Therefore, choosing a reliable team leader is important. The leader must build and maintain trust and work with others to create a healthy and productive working environment.

During my career, I learned it takes time and effort to build up a team. However, I also learnt it only takes seconds for damage to be done.

Story: I once worked with a group of incredibly intelligent, engaged, and motivated individuals. After considerable amount of effort from the team there was reason to celebrate.

Everyone was excited with the news of success. Team spirit flourished, but not for long! Management had an incredible opportunity to foster team spirit by simple acknowledgment. However, upper management sent an email to everyone congratulating one person for their role in the process. The impact of this email was deeply felt by everyone. The team spirit that was being enjoyed was suddenly destroyed. It is simply amazing how much damage one careless email can do.

Having a Diverse Team is Important

Having a team with a mixture of experience, skills, and knowledge is important.

Story: I had the pleasure of working with an MBA student on a research project. Because the research project involved a business development and retention centre, we met with their fifteen or so partners. The research project was to help identify key performance indicators and create a spreadsheet for the partners to track them. They knew their activities such as events, training sessions, and consulting work were helping, but they had no proof. They hoped the project was the solution.

Because it took greater time than expected to receive the key performance indicators from the partners, time was running out as the student needed results. Fortunately, I was able to offer my help.

Working with the student made me very aware of the importance of having a diversified team. What I could not understand, he had no problem with. What he had difficulty with, I was able to solve. I created a spreadsheet which identified the key performance indicators. We completed this project on time, and we both realized the critical importance of teamwork.

SUMMARY: PART TWO

- It is crucial to communicate to your employees that every task is important.

- If possible, allow employees to find their own way to fulfill their roles. Do not micromanage.

- Use agendas and take notes during meetings.

- Create an action item table and assign each item to an individual. Follow up to check progress before the next meeting.

- Employees will be more engaged during a meeting to discuss problems in the absence of authority figures.

- Have an open-door policy that give employees the option of speaking with you in the privacy of your office.

- Teams can be very useful in achieving results for specific projects.

PART THREE

LEADERSHIP QUALITIES

The qualities of the person providing leadership is extremely important. A leader should not take on the role to feel superior to others. Instead, a leader must have the mindset of wanting to make a difference through determined and diligent actions that will make a positive difference.

The nature and quality of leadership comes down to this reality in the workplace. Your actions speak more to the quality of your leadership than what you say. Do you respect and show consideration to all employees, or do you show favoritism? Are your employees able to approach you with their ideas without you feeling threatened?

Are you capable of thinking and planning that leads to clarity of purpose and outcomes? Do you have an organized approach to maintaining projects and workflow? Every project has three distinct parts: 1) planning, 2) implementation, and 3) evaluation and follow up of results. Should any of these not be undertaken properly, the result will be confusion, inefficiencies, and lost opportunities to learn and improve over time.

Leading by Example

An important and often overlooked role of a manager is leading by example. To develop employees who portray trust, interest, respect, and good work ethics, you need to demonstrate these qualities with consistency. If you openly demonstrate lack of trust, you will find your team will also demonstrate lack of trust. If you show up late, your team will show up late. Same goes with interest. If you show interest in your work and in the work of others, you will find your team will have greater interest in their work.

Story: Several years ago, I worked at a Research Institute who had the most incredible Director. He always came across warm, supportive, and genuinely interested in the employees, projects, and the Institute itself. When the Director retired, another Director was hired as a replacement.

The new Director came across as the complete opposite. I could not understand how such a person could be hired as a replacement. I noticed the workplace became filled with stress. It was obvious he did not care about the people and projects. This sounds bad, but being in my early twenties, when he came around...I hid!

After six months or so, an announcement was made to the employees. Unfortunately, the Research Institute was to be closed permanently! This individual had not been employed to support the Institute; he had been hired to shut it down.

Confidentiality

Building trust with employees is key to being a successful manager. When an employee discusses private or sensitive information, remember, it demonstrates that they view you as a trustful individual. Taking that information and repeating it to others can destroy that trust. Once this trust is broken, it is very difficult to mend.

In addition, you may have access to private information about employees, or information about areas of concern or upcoming changes given to you by upper management that must be confidential for various reasons until a given time. Again, be wise in what you say or write. It is important to consider the possible outcomes and consequences of speaking without thinking.

Errors are often made when one shares confidential information to a 'trusted colleague'. Always assume the information you share will eventually be leaked out. Are you willing to except responsibility if this occurs?

Problem Solving

Problems provide managers opportunities to demonstrate leadership and move forward. Take time to consider how you will respond and especially how you are going to communicate and interact with employees and stakeholders.

Problems Associated with Growth

Organizations experiencing growth will encounter new challenges and be required to solve problems that affect operations across the board as well as specific functions or parts of the organization. How we deal with problems can often move the organization forward or can result in the organization becoming stagnant at best or falling apart at worst.

Personally, I have known several entrepreneurs who worked day and night only to watch their companies fall apart once they became successful. They were not ready for the huge shift in demands and tasks required to make the transition work. The added stress also caused the partners to no longer work constructively together.

So much emphasis is placed on setting up a company with little attention on how to manage this transitional period. Managers need to come together and develop solutions to move forward through this transitional period.

If you as a front-line manager find yourself in this position, remember that you have a stake in this company. Make sure to set down and think through the changes that you believe will be necessary to help the company become successful. Consider reaching out for help as required.

Unique Problems

Problems will arise that are specifically unique and require thought and foresight from the front-line manager. They can be both challenging and exciting. These are usually individual

Leadership Qualities

occurrences, such as dealing with personnel issues. However, consideration must be given to the possibility that they can affect other areas so solutions must be comprehensive.

If you have a difficult problem, here are a few suggestions:

1. Change of environment: Often a change in environment can help you think more clearly and creatively. Consider going for a walk or going out for a coffee.

2. Seek advice or help from others: Knowing when to ask for help is a sign of strength, not weakness.

3. Web search.

4. Read books, podcasts, and blogs on the subject.

Conflict Resolution

What is conflict and how does one deal with it? Conflict infers negative issues are occurring and causing trouble in your workplace. Conflict, if not addressed, often grows worse overtime.

Conflict can cause frustration to many and can even be detrimental to the company. There are many areas that cause conflict. However, the most common are with disagreements between and among individuals. Conflict usually plays a large

Leadership Qualities

and important role in most organizations. Handling conflict puts your leadership to the test. At all times, address the situation in a professional and productive way. This will take good listening skills and careful thought.

Story: I was approached by a post-Doctorial fellow, we will call him Peter, who was visibly upset. Peter complained that another post-Doctorial fellow, we will refer to him as Bruce, had dripped water over his journal. I followed him into the lab and yes indeed there was his journal soaked with water. I then spoke to Bruce about the incident. He told me the experiment he was performing required water and therefore needed to be near the sink. I went back and noticed Peter had his personal workstation next to the sink.

It became apparent, the underlying problem was not that Bruce was careless. The real problem was the lab was not organized properly.

From this insight, shared workstations were created where individuals could go and complete a particular experiment. This also prevented people from having to search for equipment as everything required was stored at the suitable workstation.

However, using this solution resulted in another conflict situation. Sometimes individuals would forget their bottles of reagents at the shared workstations and another person would come along and use them. It occurred to me that it did not make sense for everyone to make their own solutions as it wasted valuable time. Accordingly, solutions were prepared and used by all.

This action made me aware the lab did not have standard operation procedures (SOPs). This led to all the solutions and experimental procedures having SOPs written for them. It is amazing how all this growth came from one small, seemingly insignificant, complaint!

From this experience, I learned the importance of listening to both sides of the story to get a better understanding of what is causing the conflict. Without understanding the variables, solving the conflict would be superficial at best. Another take away from this experience was to stay impartial and to be aware of growth potential opportunities.

Story: I was once helping to organize an event at a hotel. After coming into the main conference room, I quickly became aware that a hotel staff member was upset, and the volunteers were in a state of confusion. I asked what the problem was. The hotel staff member informed me one of the volunteers wanted to organize the buffet incorrectly and refused to listen to her. I was amazed and surprised that a person with no experience would not take the advice of professional hotel staff. Because we had over 200 event attendees about to come through the doors, I quickly took over and told the other volunteers to follow the hotel staff's directions.

Afterwards, I did not feel good about how I dealt with the individual. The buffet had gotten organized and was successful, but I felt badly because I could have taught the volunteer a valuable life lesson. After the event, I should have discussed the situation with him and explained how it is important to take advice and listen to experts. I expect the experience only left him with bad feelings and a damaged ego.

Leadership Qualities

Do We Understand Each Other

Conflicts often result due to misunderstandings. We live in a multicultural environment where misunderstanding can occur more frequently due to language and cultural differences.

Using clear and concise language will help reduce the probability of conflict. It is also important to take the time to make sure your audience understands.

When dealing with conflict, there are times when some areas are best not to get involved in depending on their severity. If there is ongoing conflict between or among staff, then it is time for a discussion. The first step is to encourage them to meet and discuss the issue or issues. If the conflict continues, then Human Resources should be notified to help rectify the problem.

Workplace Protocols

A workplace protocol is a system of rules that articulates and explains the correct conduct and procedures to be followed in specific situations. For example, organizations have specific labour laws and regulations, especially when dealing with safety, that you need to be aware of and keep updated for changes. To ensure these requirements are being followed and implemented is often done through specified protocols. All protocols, regardless of the reason for them, must result in desired outcomes.

To be an effective leader requires the front-line manager to acknowledge and experiment with new ideas when previous protocols need to be updated. This is best achieved through good communication with your staff. Their suggestions and acceptance will help both you and them to get them right.

An example is sick leave. I use sick leave to show how sick leave protocols can be managed to make a difference. I had the opportunity to witness how a manager deals with sick leave can have a noticeable effect on the employees and company.

When working at a university, I noticed absences due to sickness were occurring frequently. The duration was from one day to one week. I decided to change how we responded to illness. At a team meeting I suggested that when someone started to feel sick, they should stay at home and rest.

I felt if we simply acknowledged this and stayed home to rest, this would prevent people from becoming full blown sick and would prevent the spread to their colleagues.

Perhaps it was purely by chance, but the number of days taken for sick leave reduced significantly. The team had accepted the idea and followed it.

I would like to have the opportunity to test this theory out properly by having people follow this concept and recording the pre sick leave taken compared with post sick leave taken based on past practices.

In my opinion, this should be the normal protocol for people taking sick leave. Forcing people to work when they are ill is not productive, causing longer periods of sickness, spread of sickness to their colleagues, and goes against creating a trusting and caring environment.

To Err is to be Human

In the workplace, we are often rewarded to play it safe and minimize the risk of making a mistake. This can have the effect of blocking creativity and making us think twice before we attempt anything new.

Regardless of where you work, the reality is that errors and mistakes will occur. To be an effective leader, acknowledge that mistakes will occur. How you handle both your own mistakes and those of your employees are especially important.

You can needlessly cause stress and anxiety both to yourself and your employees, or you can choose to use the errors as opportunities for potential growth.

Story: During the early years of my career in science, I noticed if errors were made, individuals would quickly hide them and pretend they never happened. To change this, I spoke openly about errors, making it part of my welcoming speech when new employees came into the lab.

The "talk" explained how everyone makes mistakes. They happen to everyone! It is part of being human. What is important is how we deal with errors and what we learn in the process. It is worth pointing out that many important discoveries came from errors or accidents.

My favorite example is how Sir Alexander Fleming discovered penicillin. Fleming in 1928, a young bacteriologist working at St. Mary's Hospital in London, left petri dishes on the bench containing colonies of Staphylococcus (S) aureus. When he came back from vacation, he and his research scholar Daniel Merlin Pryce noticed one of the petri dishes had lost its

Leadership Qualities

cover. On the dish appeared a blue-green mould. They noticed in the area with the mold growth, the S aureus colonies had died.

It is important to note that Fleming's discovery would have never caused the revolution in medicine if he and Pryce had not continued with experiments with the mold and published their results. It took another twelve years until Howard Florey and Ernest Chain turned the discovery of penicillin into a usable product.

Going back to the lab story...I told individuals, if they make a mistake, to write down their error and continue with the experiment. The results were to be recorded along with the error that brought about the result. In addition, they were instructed to write what they might do next time, to prevent the error from re-occurring. This practice allowed them to make the error a learning opportunity and possibly a discovery.

Taking Responsibility

When an error occurs, the best practice is to take responsibility for it. Tell your employees to always tell those who are affected by it. This is also true for the front-line manager. Telling others of your mistake will encourage your employees to do the same.

There will be times when taking responsibility for an error, does not mean having to broadcast it to colleagues, or even the manager should they not be affected. However, you or your staff need to acknowledge the error, fix it, and learn how to prevent a recurrence.

Leadership Qualities

As a front-line manager there will likely be times when errors are made which make you angry. However, if you feel angry it is a time to stop and consider how to handle the situation without making matters worse. Scolding, yelling, or threatening an employee will only cause more stress and anxiety which in turn may lead to further mistakes by the employee.

Some circumstances can be difficult, and any manager or person can react before thinking. Taking three deep breaths before speaking and waiting until you can think clearly without intense emotion is important. If you do react inappropriately, apologize once you have had time to reflect and calm down.

Your team members do not expect you to be super-human, however, acknowledging your error of overreacting, demonstrates that you are indeed human, and you take responsibility for your actions.

Taking this action shows you not only teach but you also practice what you teach. This regains trust and deepens relationships within the group.

If you need to discuss errors with an employee, do so in private. Identify the errors and ask the employee to explain why they happen and how they can prevent them from re-occurring. Also be open to discussion, a sudden emergence of errors could be due to personal issues such as a divorce, death of a loved one, a new family member, etc. We all go through times in our lives where we struggle.

QUESTIONS FOR REFLECTION

Leadership Qualities

1. What is the most difficult problem you have faced as a manager?

2. What was the response you took to address the problem?

3. In what ways did you demonstrate leadership in facing problems?

4. How would you describe outcomes in terms of solving the problem?

5. How would you describe outcomes in terms of building capabilities and commitment on the part of your employees?

SUMMARY: PART THREE

- Lead by example.

- Problems provide managers opportunities to demonstrate leadership.

- Exercise patience and listen to all sides when resolving conflicts. Identify underlying causes and look for solutions.

- Experiment and seek new ideas from employees when updating workplace protocols.

- Encourage employees to acknowledge and learn from mistakes.

- Remember to practice what you tell employees.

- Trust is a two-way street. Listen to your employees and acknowledge their input.

PART FOUR

PERSONAL DEVELOPMENT

Work Life Balance

Having a proper work life balance is challenging as we are now connected by our cell phones and the internet. This makes it more difficult to make a complete transition between work and home life. To be healthy individuals, we need to find balance between our work and personal lives. As a front-line manager you need to nurture this healthy balance in your personal life while at the same time encouraging your employees along this path.

Personal Development

Story: During my career I worked at a Research Institute where I enjoyed the work so much, I would leave for dinner and would often come back and work into the night. When the weekends came, I was disappointed because the building was closed. When my supervisor found out I was coming back in the evenings, she was rather concerned.

Her intervention reminded me that I did need more in my personal life. To fill the gap, I joined a swimming club, movie club, and took a pottery class. From these activities, I met people and learned that making pottery is a lot harder than it looks!

This experience helped me to discover that developing and sustaining relationships and activities outside of my work was necessary as I began to enjoy a more balanced life.

Now later in life with a family, I also realize the importance of being emotionally present with those around me and not just physically present.

Possible Solutions

More and more, we find ourselves responding to our mobile phone's constant need for attention informing us when we have an email, text message, etc.

If you find you are spending too much time on your phone, you might consider taking back control of how you choose to spend your time. I believe, for the most part, we are letting our phones manage our time. You can change this by managing your time accordingly.

Set aside time when you will not be responsive to your calls, emails, texts, and more. Make this happen by setting aside the phone and turning off notifications.

Doing so will provide us with a more balanced life both for our families and ourselves. Try to remember that making time every day to spend with your loved ones is important.

Overcoming Stage Fright

Speaking in public often frightens people. It makes one feel insecure to know that a group of people will be listening to every word one speaks. For many individuals this is challenging, and it can cause extreme anxiety.

As a front-line manager, there will be times when you might have to speak at team meetings or undertake presentations to your employees or to upper management. This could be perceived as an opportunity to share their knowledge while at the same time frightening. What if your performance is judged harshly by others? What if you make a mistake?

Story: Growing up I was very shy, and this continued even through college. This shyness affected my thinking and my performance.

One of the mandatory courses in my program was Report Writing. Unfortunately, after completing the report, we had to stand up and present it to the class. Terrified, my fear of public speaking controlled me. I simply refused even if it meant failing. Indeed, I did fail! I received an incomplete grade and took the class over again.

This time picking a topic that I found remarkably interesting, and with some fear and trembling I was able to stand up and present in front of the class. The fear that I experienced did not stop me from trying.

Throughout my career, I have slowly improved. I now speak in front of groups, host workshops, and have even been an MC at a conference.

This became possible through practice and patience. I also had advice from a consultant with whom I had the pleasure to learn and work with. He told me to take three deep breaths before going up to speak. It is amazing how quickly the nervous system reacts when you do this simple but effective technique. Accordingly, I recommend this to any speaker who experiences anxiety.

In hindsight, I would have progressed faster and far better if I had sought help, such as joining Toastmasters. This is an international non-profit organization focused on developing communication, public speaking, and leadership skills. I know several individuals who, after joining the Toastmasters Club, reported that their skills improved considerably.

For more information on Toastmasters, please visit:

https://www.toastmasters.org/

Opportunities For Improvement

Opportunities for growth should be offered whenever possible for both you and your staff. Doing this will help bring new knowledge and skills into your workplace. Employees often see this as a welcome opportunity for personal growth and improvement. This in turn should bring about improvement in performance and to your organization.

Taking advantage of opportunities however can easily be overlooked when we become focused on our daily routines. The following are examples of growth opportunities for both you and your employees.

Additional Training

Attending regular training sessions will help keep individuals open to learning and flexible to change and new ideas. Having a mixture of training such as communication, technical, management, team building, etc., helps to maintain a learning state of mind.

If funds are limited for training, consider sending one or two employees. They can then host a training session for the rest of your employees. The following are examples of helpful workshops.

- Communication skill training
- Technical training
- Problem solving
- Stress management

Conferences

Attending conferences is an excellent way to stay current in your field. In addition, attending conferences presents us with an opportunity to network with other individuals with similar interests. Having the opportunity to present at a conference provides a unique opportunity to share your knowledge and talk about your organization and project.

Reading

Consider reading as an opportunity for improvement. Keep updated on any new laws and regulations that could affect your area of expertise. Research papers are another area where you can find advanced information. Magazines and newspapers can also contain valuable information that could be useful. Sharing information that is of value to your employees is also a good practice.

Collaborating

If opportunities occur that allows for collaborating on projects with other departments or organizations, consider them. Collaborations present excellent learning opportunities. Learning from others is powerful and they too, can learn from you. Accordingly, if possible, allow staff to participate where it is in the best interest of your organization to do so.

Participating in Publications

Participating in publications may open a path to share expertise that could help others and help your company. This also could lead to improvements in writing and thinking skills for the authors.

Extending your or your employees' expertise within the organization, outside of normal responsibilities

This could be joining a team, creating a presentation for a conference, learning a new skill, or passing on skills to others.

Managing Stress

Stress is a human reaction that happens to us all. Our bodies are designed to experience stress and react to it. Stress can be positive, keeping us alert and ready to avoid danger. However, managing stress in our daily lives is important for both you and your employees.

Stress is part of everyday life, and it results from both positive and negative changes in our lives. It occurs as we rush to get ready and out the door in the morning. Stress is present when we step onto an overcrowded bus, or when we find ourselves in a traffic jam knowing we will be late for an important meeting. Stress is a given but how we deal with stress is important.

As the front-line manager, you can either create or reduce the level of stress in the environment. If you come into work stressed, you will have a negative impact on the people around you. If you come to work relaxed, confident with a clear mind, you will have a positive impact.

How do we control our stress levels?

There are many excellent books available on managing stress, and I encourage you to seek one out if you feel your stress level is having a negative impact on you or people in your life.

Using techniques to manage stress can bring significant benefits to your personal life, your career, your employees, and the organization.

Personal Development

The following are a few methods that I have learnt to help manage stress:

Work Related:

- Have a clear understanding of your role in the organization, including your upward reporting responsibilities.
- Get to know your employees – each person is different.
- Avoid showing favoritism.
- Be assertive.
- Set realistic goals and expectations for yourself and others.
- Reduce your stress before coming into work.

Health Related:

- Eat healthy.
- Get enough sleep.
- Exercise regularly.
- Spend time with family and friends.
- Spend time in nature.
- Drink alcoholic beverages in moderation.
- Practice relaxation techniques, such as meditation, listen to soothing music, and visualization exercises.
- Avoid going against your values.
- Read.

Personal Experience

From personal experience, I found all the following to have a positive influence on the level of stress in the workplace:

- Limit the amount of change occurring at any given time.
- Clearly define roles, responsibilities, and expectations for your employees.
- Give individuals control on how they accomplish their tasks.
- Plan for required resources.
- Solve problems and conflicts as they arrive.
- Delegate jobs.
- Be a good listener.
- Have an open-door policy.
- Encourage work life balance for your employees and yourself.
- Hold meetings as needed and keep them focused.
- Work everyday to build and maintain trust.

If you feel help is needed, consider **counselling**. Counselling can allow one to recognize the sources of stress and help identify stress management techniques that are most suitable for your level of health and lifestyle.

Personal Development

QUESTIONS FOR REFLECTION

1. What are three personal development goals you would like to pursue?

2. How could these personal development goals contribute to your life outside of work? How could they help you become a better manager?

3. What do you feel is the main sources of stress in your workplace?

Personal Development

SUMMARY: PART FOUR

- Promote a healthy work-life balance.

- Taking three deep breaths helps to lower stress and anxiety.

- Joining a Toastmasters Club can help with public speaking and with leadership skills.

- Keep aware of possible individual growth opportunities.

- Become a good listener. Encourage your employees to discuss ideas or issues with you.

- Handling stress is important to you, your employees, and the organization.

Conclusion

Employing the right management approach can have an incredible impact, for the front-line manager, the company, and in the lives of the individuals they employ.

The points mentioned in this book are meant to encourage and assist the front-line manager to engage with all levels of managers and their employees with integrity and consideration. The principal outcome is to create productivity while fostering a healthy and supportive work environment. Not surprisingly, these are also key elements which will reduce stress in the workplace.

I believe that any workplace can be a place of security, but often, it is not, mainly due to lapses in understanding basic knowledge on very important concepts. I end this book by suggesting that you remember the following key points:

1. Clearly define roles and responsibilities.
2. Allow employees to ask questions about their work practices and the work environment.
3. Create a culture of continuous improvement.
4. Keep an open mind and adapt to changing circumstances and needs.
5. Take the time to solve issues in a fair and researched manner.
6. Reach out to others to gain advice and access resources when needed.

I wish you well on your journey!

www.ingramcontent.com/pod-product-compliance
Lightning Source LLC
Chambersburg PA
CBHW030044100526
44590CB00011B/331